MY PET
RaT

**Elizabeth
Simon**

WEIGL PUBLISHERS INC.
"Creating Inspired Learning"
www.weigl.com

Published by Weigl Publishers Inc.
350 5th Avenue, 59th Floor
New York, NY 10118
Website: www.weigl.com

Project Coordinator
Heather C. Hudak

Design
Terry Paulhus

Library of Congress Cataloging-in-Publication Data available upon request.
Fax 1-866-44-WEIGL for the attention of the Publishing Records department.

ISBN 978-1-61690-079-3 (hard cover)
ISBN 978-1-61690-080-9 (soft cover)

Printed in the United States of America in North Mankato, Minnesota
1 2 3 4 5 6 7 8 9 0   14 13 12 11 10

052010
WEP264000

Photograph and Text Credits

Contents

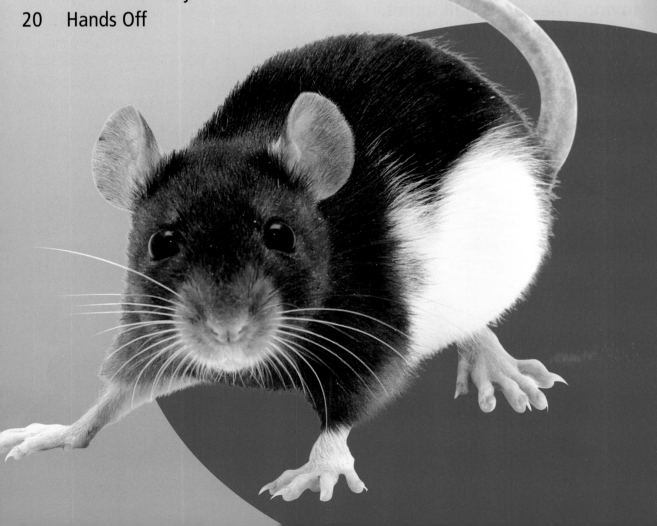

Rat Rants

For thousands of years, people have feared and even hated rats. Today, many people are not afraid of **domesticated** rats. These animals make great pets. Rats are active, curious, and loving. They are small, quiet, and very clean. They do not require space, and they never need to be walked. Rats love to climb, hide, and play. They can even be taught to do tricks.

Do not buy a rat that squeaks when it is touched. These rats have not been handled often.

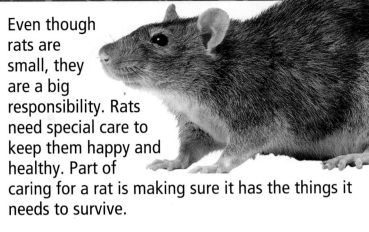

Even though rats are small, they are a big responsibility. Rats need special care to keep them happy and healthy. Part of caring for a rat is making sure it has the things it needs to survive.

Rats need plenty of food and water, a comfortable place to live, and attention. Each rat has its own **personality**. It is important that you get to know your rat so you can care for it properly. Like humans, rats have certain likes and dislikes. If you take the time to learn what those are, your rat will return your love. It will be a fun and playful pet.

fancy facts

- Male rats are called "bucks." Female rats are called "does." Baby rats are called "kittens."
- A rat's tail is often the same length as its body.
- Most rats live to be about three years old.
- Some pet rats are called fancy rats. These rats meet special rat club standards. For example, they may have wavy fur or short tails.

Pet Profiles

Pet rats are not divided into **breeds**. They are organized by variety, or type, instead. Rats may have different colors or markings. They come in a variety of colors, including beige, black, brown, and gray. Some varieties have special body features. They may have straight or wavy fur, for example. Others may have long or short tails.

Siamese

- Has dark patches of fur around its nose, tail, and paws, which are similar to the markings a Siamese cat
- Makes a very good pet
- New related species called the "triamese," which has three colors of fur, was introduced by breeders in the United States

Peach Self

- Has solid-colored fur with no other markings
- Belly fur may be a slightly paler color
- Ranges in color from black to white, blue, chocolate, lilac, and silver

DUMBO

- Comes in many colors with different markings
- Has large, wide ears on the sides of its head
- Has a flatter head than other breeds
- Very calm; good-natured
- Named for the cartoon character Dumbo because their large ears look like elephant ears

MANX

- Comes in many colors with different markings
- Also called the tailless rat
- First bred in England in 1915 by scientist Geoff Izzard, who thought that people did not like owning pet rats because of their long, hairless tails
- Has longer, more angled legs to help keep its balance

HAIRLESS

- No fur and smooth skin
- First hairless rat was called a nude rat; was born to furry parents in a laboratory
- Requires more care than other rats; becomes cold and ill very easily

HOODED

- Has a dark head, neck, chest, and shoulders, and a white body with a long stripe along its spine
- Comes in many colors, such as chocolate, cream, and fawn
- Body shape is either standard or dumbo

Rat Report

Rats have lived on Earth for millions of years. Rats were once feared creatures. They have been well-loved pets since the late 1700s. People hunted and trapped **albino** rats, which were born to common brown rats, because they liked their snow-white fur and pink eyes. Over time, people discovered that rats are very smart and can be tamed. Scientists and **fanciers** found ways to breed different types of rats that people could keep as pets.

Albinos were the first type of rat to be commonly kept as pets. Some albino rats have white bodies and pink eyes.

Two types of rats are found in most parts of the world. These are the brown rat and the black rat. The black rat was brought to North America in the 1600s. It lives in tropical and subtropical America and the southern United States.

The brown rat was brought to the United States from Europe in the 1800s. The brown rat is the most common rat in the United States. It is larger than the black rat. The brown rat can survive in harsher environments.

Rat Report

- Murids are the ancestors of brown rats and house mice.
- One reason people feared rats was because of a terrible **plague**, or disease, that killed millions of people in the 1300s. People believed the disease was spread through rat bites.

In fact, it was fleas living in the rats' fur that spread the disease.
- Rats are related to other members of the rodent family, including gerbils and squirrels. Rodents are the largest group of **mammals** in the world. They have long front teeth.

9

Life Cycle

It is exciting to bring home a cute, tiny rat from the pet store. Throughout its lifetime, your pet rat will depend on you for food, shelter, and love. Rats live between two and three years. Like all pets, a rat's needs will change during its lifetime.

Newborn Rat

Newborn rats are slightly larger than a penny. They have no hair, and they cannot see. They are completely helpless. They must depend on their mother for food and protection. Rats grow very quickly.

After five days, newborn rats have some fur and can crawl. They do not open their eyes until they are two weeks old. If they crawl out of the nest, they cannot find their way back. Their mother must find them.

Four Weeks

At four weeks old, rats no longer need their mothers to care for them. They are alert, curious, and can feed themselves. They are also ready to leave their mothers and be taken home. Rats can be **adopted** at any age, but at four weeks old, they are easier to train. They can also get to know and trust their owners more quickly.

One Year

One-year-old rats are fully grown. They have developed their own personalities. Rats are considered adults at one year of age. Adult rats are very active. They enjoy playing in and out of their cages. They like to climb, run on wheels, and catch bits of string that are dangled in front of them.

More Than One Year

As rats age, they become less active. Many develop hearing and sight problems. They also cannot climb or play as well as they once could. Still, older rats need a great deal of love and attention.

Rug Rats

- Female rats give birth to between eight and 20 kittens at one time.
- Rats can have as many as 200 kittens in one year.
- Female rats can have kittens when they are as young as five weeks old.
- Some rats live to be 5 years old. Scientists in the United States are looking for ways to lengthen rats' lives. This will allow people to enjoy their furry friends for longer periods of time.

Picking Your Pet

Deciding to own and care for a pet is a big responsibility. Read, research, and talk to pet owners before you decide which pet is right for you. Before you make the trip to the pet store, ask yourself some important questions.

If you are adding another rat to your cage, keep the new rat separate for at least two to three weeks to prevent spreading disease.

What Will a Rat Cost?

Most rat types do not cost much to buy. Some rat varieties, such as dumbo and manx, cost more. Although rats are inexpensive, setting up a cage or enclosure and buying supplies can be costly. Pet rat supplies, such as food, bedding material, and toys, are regular expenses. Rats should also visit a **veterinarian** once each year. If your rat becomes ill, you may need to buy it medication, too.

What Do I Have Time For?

Rats do not need to live in pairs or groups, but most prefer companionship, especially from other rats. They also need their owner's time and attention every day. Can you take care of more than one pet? Can you give your pet or pets the time they need? Rats are very friendly, but they must be handled frequently to make sure they do not become afraid of people. Rats do not need to be **groomed**, but their cage needs to be cleaned often. They need fresh food and water at least once each day.

How Will a Rat Affect My Family?

It is very important to find out how the members of your family feel about your new pet. Some people are frightened of rats. Some people are also **allergic** to rats. This can cause serious health problems for people in your home. Think about other pets in your household, too. Some cats and dogs live well with rats. Others may try to harm or catch the rat.

Rodent Restrictions

- In some places, it is illegal to own a pet rat.
- In nature, rats sometimes eat small animals. If you have a pet rat, you must keep it away from other pets, such as hamsters, gerbils, fish, and birds.
- There are about 1.25 billion rats in the United States. About 3.5 million rats are born every day around the world.
- Rats found in nature do not make good pets. These rats are very aggressive. Buy your pet rat from a breeder or pet store.

Rat Rations

Before bringing home a pet rat, make sure you have the right supplies. Rats need a large home with a warm, dark place to sleep. They require food dishes, a water bottle, and toys they can climb for exercise. Rats love to chew things, so the best homes are metal cages or large aquariums.

Rats are very sensitive to light and heat. Be sure to keep their cages away from direct sunlight. They should also be kept away from radiators or drafts.

Cages or aquariums must be lined with hay or **pellets**. These items can be bought at any pet store. This bottom layer of bedding helps keep rats warm and clean. Rats love to make nests. A store-bought home or a box with a hole cut into it should be placed in the cage or aquarium. Fill the box with shredded paper, paper towel, or fabric so the rats can nest.

Aquariums must be well **ventilated**. They should have wire mesh lids so the rats can breathe and do not get too hot. There should be 15 to 20 gallons (56.8 to 75.7 liters) of tank space for each rat living in the aquarium. Wire cages should have a plastic or metal pan on the bottom that can be lined with bedding. There should be about 2 cubic feet (0.06 cubic meters) of space per rat inside the cage.

Modern Living

- Rats divide their cages into separate areas for going to the washroom, sleeping, and playing, like humans do in their homes.
- Wire floors can cause foot problems for your pet rat, so the floors on all levels of the cage should be solid.

- Rats may have difficulty breathing around wood chips or shavings. Do not use these items to line a cage.

Rat Refreshments

Rats will eat anything. They need a combination of pet store food and fresh foods such as fruits and vegetables. Rats love fresh vegetables such as broccoli, carrots, and shelled peas. They can have vegetables every day. Rats also enjoy eating fruits such as strawberries, bananas, and apples. Only give your rat fruit as a treat. Too much fruit can cause an upset stomach.

Clean, fresh water should be available for your rat at all times.

How Much Food Should I Give My Rat?

Pet stores, books, and veterinarians can recommend how much to feed a rat, but it is important that you pay attention to what works best for your pet. Notice if your rat never finishes his or her food or gets sick from certain fresh foods. You can change the amount and type of food you feed your rat to make sure he or she is as healthy as possible.

Gourmet Grazing

- Rats love people food. They can have white bread, noodles, cooked egg, or fish as a special treat.
- Rats never burp or vomit. One reason they can eat so many different foods is because they have a very strong stomach.
- Rats enjoy eating junk food such as potato chips and cake. These foods do not provide the proper nutrition rats need to be healthy.
- Many people believe rats like cheese. Actually, rats are allergic to cheese.

Small and Furry

Whether wild or tame, most rats have common features. Their fur keeps them warm and dry. Their long tails help them keep their balance while climbing. They also use their tails to find their way around their surroundings. These features help rats survive.

 7 Essential Parts of the Rat

A rat's long tail is part of its backbone, which helps it balance. The fine hairs on its tail are very sensitive and help the rat feel its way around in the dark.

Rats have short fur that helps keep them warm. They also have long fur that protects their skin.

Rats have very keen hearing. Humans cannot hear some of the sounds rats use to communicate.

Rats have very flexible front paws, which they use to clean themselves and eat. Rats use their tiny fingers to peel fruit, seeds, and nuts before eating them.

Rats cannot see very well. They have stiff, sensitive whiskers that help rats feel their way through tight spaces.

Rats need a keen sense of smell to find food. Rats can tell by the way a person or animal smells whether it is a friend or enemy.

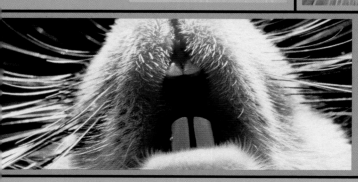

A rat's incisors, or long front teeth, are used to break through hard shells and nuts. They also **gnaw** through wood and other materials. Rats use their molars, or large flat teeth, to chew and grind their food into smaller pieces.

Hands Off

Rats' cages need to be cleaned often. Owners should remove and replace the soiled bedding in their rat's cage every day. They should then add about 2 to 3 inches (5.1 to 7.6 centimeters) of new bedding. Cages need to be emptied, scrubbed, and dried once each week. Use soapy water, and be sure to rinse well. This will keep the cage free of germs that can make rats sick.

Rats are clean animals, so they like clean cages.

Rats spend nearly one-third of their lives cleaning and grooming their fur, ears, face, and tail. This means they do not need to be groomed by their owners. Rats can be bathed if they become smelly, which is rare, or if they get fleas. Special shampoo can be bought at pet stores. This shampoo is very mild. It will not hurt rats' skin or strip the oils in their fur.

Rats' teeth never stop growing. Rats cannot eat if their teeth grow too long. They can develop scabs and sores around their mouth, too. Veterinarians can trim rat's teeth. Rats can chew things to grind their teeth down, too.

Respectable Rodents

- Rats spend more time grooming than most other animals, including cats.
- Rat owners should trim their pet's claws often. One person should hold the rat, while another person clips its claws.

Be careful not to clip too close to the **quick**. This will cause bleeding. If the quick is cut, use corn starch to stop any bleeding.
- Many rats love to swim. They can hold their breath underwater for up to three minutes.

Healthy and Happy

Keeping your rat healthy will keep it happy. Healthy rats are playful and friendly. They enjoy human contact. If a rat is ill, it may not want to be held or play. The rat may stay at the back of its cage. The veterinarian can answer your questions or help if your pet becomes ill. It is important to choose a veterinarian who has experience with rats.

Rats do not enjoy living alone. They may become bored and develop behavior and health problems.

If you choose to own more than one rat, it is important to talk to your veterinarian about **neutering** or **spaying**. These operations keep male rats from fighting and female rats from having kittens.

Once you know your rat's personality, you will be able to tell if it is not well. Is your rat sleeping more or less than usual? Have the rat's eating habits changed? Is the rat limping or moving more slowly than usual? As rats get older, they are prone to certain illnesses.

Once each week, check for redness around the rat's nose and eyes. This is a sign that the rat may have an eye infection due to injury, dust, or illness. Check for scabs on the rat's body. Scabs on the rat's chin and around its whiskers may be caused by too much **protein** in its diet. Mites look like scabs around the outside of the ears. The rat may have a respiratory infection if it is sneezing often or breathing loudly. These are just a few of the symptoms rats have when they are ill. Keep a watchful eye on your pet, and take it to the veterinarian if you think it is not well.

Queasy Critters

- Some rats will stare in the air and sway to help them see better. This behavior is most common in pink-eyed rats.

- If a rat walks with its head tilted, it may have an ear infection. Rats tilt their heads when they cannot hear properly.

Rat Behavior

When you bring your rat home, it is important to let him get to know you. Rats are very small compared to people. The rat might be scared of your size and smell at first. Each day, put your hand into the rat's cage. Over time, the rat will become more comfortable with you. Soon, you will be able to pick up your pet rat.

Pet rats will let their owners know if they want to be picked up. Never pull a rat out of its home or cage. Use one hand to support the rat's bottom. Place your other hand over the rat's back. Pet rats enjoy being held, cuddled, and petted. Some rats may even climb on your arm or shoulder.

You must supervise your rat if you let it outside of its cage. Make sure it does not chew on electrical cords or become trapped behind furniture.

24

It is important to hold and play with your rat every day. Though rats cannot speak and they rarely make any sounds, you can learn to communicate with your pet. You can tell how your rat is feeling by the way it reacts when you hold it. Rats enjoy living in pairs or groups. It is best to house two females or two males in the same cage. The pair will get plenty of exercise playing together.

They will enjoy grooming each other and sleeping together in a pile, too. Happy rats may even try grooming their owners by licking their fingers or hair.

Pet Peeves

Rats do not like:
- loud noises
- being too hot or too cold
- having their tails pulled
- being in direct sunlight
- too much fruit

Readjusted Rats

- Rats are very smart and can be trained. Some rats respond when their names are called. Others can be taught to find their way out of **mazes**.
- Rats are **nocturnal**, which means they are mainly active at night. They can be trained to be active during the day.
- When rats are happy, they chatter or grind their teeth together. This is called "bruxing."

Rat Tales

The best-known folk tale about rats is the *The Pied Piper of Hamelin*. It is the story of a man who is hired to lure a group of pesky rats away from the town of Hamelin. Similar folk tales are told in France, Austria, and China.

Some people believe *The Pied Piper of Hamelin* is a true story.

Rat Ramblings

"The Sagacious Rat" is one of Aesop's Fables. It is about a rat who does not want to be eaten by a hungry cat. The rat invites another rat to join him on a journey. He tells his friend that he planned to travel alone, but he really wanted to spend time with his friend. The friend agrees to join the rat. The friend suggests the rat lead the way, but the rat refuses, saying his friend should lead. Delighted, the friend leads the way. The friend leaves the hole first and is caught by the cat. The cat runs away with the rat's friend. The rat walks away without being noticed by the cat.

Taken from Aesop's Fables

Rats have been kept as pets for a few hundred years. Some well-known people have called rats their friends. President Theodore Roosevelt had three pet rats, including one named Jonathan. Author Beatrix Potter had a pet rat named Sammy.

Rats have appeared in movies, books, television shows, stories, and fables. The rats in Robert C. O'Brien's popular book *Mrs. Frisby and the Rats of NIMH* help Mrs. Frisby, a mouse who lives with the rats on the Fitzgibbon Farm, tend to her sick son.

Rizzo the rat is a popular character on *The Muppet Show*. Rizzo appears in many episodes of the television show. He also appears in the Muppet movies. Rizzo is often a stagehand or narrator.

Revered Rodents

- Rats have been important characters in movies, including *Babe* and *Chicken Run*. They have also been in books, such as *Charlotte's Web* and the Harry Potter series.

- In China, rats are worshiped because they are believed to bring good luck and fortune.

Pet Puzzlers

What do you know about rats? If you can answer the following questions correctly, you may be ready to own a rat.

Q How often does a rat's cage need cleaning?

A Remove soiled wood chips and bedding from the rat's cage every day. Wood chips and all bedding should be replaced once a week. The entire cage should be cleaned once a month to prevent germs from building up.

Q What is the best kind of cage for a pet rat?

A Rats need a metal cage or an aquarium that they cannot chew through. Aquariums must be well ventilated to make sure rats have enough air and do not get too hot.

Q What do rats use their tails for?

A Rats use their tales to help them balance and feel their way around in the dark.

Q How long have people kept rats as pets?

A People have kept rats as pets since the 1700s.

Q What can a veterinarian do if your rat's teeth grow too long?

A A veterinarian can trim your rat's teeth to make sure it can eat properly.

Q What should you feed your rat?

A You can feed your rat a mixture of pet store and fresh foods, such as vegetables and meat.

Q How can you tell when your rat is happy?

A Rats chatter or grind their teeth when they are happy.

Rat Raves

Before you buy your pet rat, write down some rat names that you like. Some names may work better for a female rat. Others may suit a male rat. Here are just a few suggestions.

Ratty

Curly

Scamp

Rosy

Rizzo

Patch

Dot

Rogue

Scabbers

Badger

Frequently Asked Questions

Should I buy a male or female rat?

Most experts agree that there is little difference between the personalities of male and female rats. The most important thing to remember is that if you get more than one rat, you should make sure they are both males or females.

Why does my rat chew everything? Should I try to stop it?

Rats need to chew things to make sure their teeth do not grow too long. Rats' teeth are so strong they can chew through wood, metal, and even concrete. To make sure your rat is not chewing things you do not want it to, you can buy special blocks of wood to keep the rat busy gnawing.

Should I groom my pet rat?

Rats spend a great deal of time cleaning and grooming their fur, ears, face, and tail. This means they do not need to be groomed. Rats can be bathed if they become smelly, which is rare, or if they get fleas.

More Information

Animal Organizations

You can help rats stay healthy and happy by learning more about them. Many organizations are dedicated to teaching people how to care for and protect their pet pals. For more rat information, write to the following organizations.

American Fancy Rat and Mouse Association (AFRMA)
9230 64th Street
Riverside, CA 92509-5924

Rat and Mouse Club of America (RMCA)
9082 Modoc Road
Westminster, CA 92683

Websites

To answer more of your rat questions, go online, and surf to the following websites.

American Fancy Rat and Mouse Association (AFRMA)
www.afrma.org

Rat & Mouse Club of America (RMCA)
www.rmca.org

The Humane Society of the United States
www.hsus.org

Words to Know

adopted: to legally take into one's own family and raise as one's own

albino: an animal that has no pigment, or color, in its skin, fur, or eyes

allergic: sensitive to specific items, which may cause sneezing, itching, and rashes

breeds: groups of animals that share specific characteristics

domesticated: tamed and used to living among people

fanciers: people who breed an animal to have certain features

gnaw: to bite, nibble, or chew

groomed: cleaned by removing dirt from fur

mammals: warm-blooded animals that feed their young milk they produce themselves

mazes: groups of paths or passageways that ar confusing to get through

neutering: making male animals unable to reproduce

nocturnal: most active at night

pellets: small pieces of material

personality: individual behaviors

plague: a disease

protein: a substance found in all living things that is needed for survival

quick: sensitive skin under nails or claws

spaying: making female animals unable to reproduce

ventilated: equipped with openings through which fresh air can pass

veterinarian: animal doctor

Index